PRECIOUS MOMENTS With Dick and Jane

Written by Roseann Woodka, PhD
Illustrated by Elena Bogatireva

Precious Moments with Dick and Jane was inspired by the true story of the beginning of Dick and Jane's lives. Each vignette depicts real antics of these abandoned, and subsequently, rescued puppies.

The book is divided into three sections: The Beginning; The View from the Office; and The Clients. The format of this book is in individual vignettes. It can be started and stopped according to the attention span and interest of the child.

The ending of *Precious Moments with Dick and Jane* identifies values that children can learn through the eyes and behaviors of puppies: Hope, Loyalty, Fun, Love, Empathy, Friendship, Happiness, Humor, and Respect. It is my hope that the reader and the child can incorporate these values into their own lives.

Second and third books, *Double Trouble with Dick and Jane* and *Senior Living with Dick and Jane* will be formatted in the same way. They will demonstrate similar values through different vignettes.

I hope you will enjoy reading *Precious Moments with Dick and Jane*.

TRIBUTE

To Jenny Cooper—the "nice lady" who brought joy and happiness to my life.

WORDS FROM JENNY COOPER

"Nice Lady"

"I will never forget that night."

"They were soaking wet when I found them. They were in a box all wet from the rain, covered with dirt, and were very stinky.

It was so sad. It was cold that night. They were shaking and huddled together. They were so loving and loved getting a warm bath.

They didn't even whine that first night.

Such a sad story, but such an amazing life they have now."

Every puppy has a story, but we have an extra special story. It's about mischief, sweetness and love.

It starts at the beginning of our lives. Well, almost the beginning. Mommy said we were about 10 weeks old when we came into her life.

The Beginning

Someone had dropped us off outside a place for lost doggies, but it was all locked up. We were huddled together in a cardboard box. We were shivering and whimpering and VERY scared. It was really cold, rainy and dark. We didn't know where our doggie mommy was. We had been staying with a human mommy. I guess she couldn't keep us even though we were really sweet and cute.

We heard a car stopping so we picked our heads up hoping the driver would find us. We barked and cried at the same time, and the lady in the car heard us.

Animal Shelter

closed

The lady peered into the box. She was surprised when she saw us. She swooped us up, wrapped us together in a warm blanket, and took us to her house. She was really nice.

We were hungry and VERY stinky. She fed us and gave us our very first bath.

We heard the nice lady tell someone that she found us on her way home from seeing a movie, *Fun with Dick and Jane*. She must have named us after the movie because she kept calling us "Dick and Jane". Mommy later told us that she and her friends learned to read from books that had OUR names!

The nice lady had just rescued a dog of her own, and she could not keep us. That made one doggie mommy and two human mommies who could not keep us. We were so sad.

The next day, on our way back to the place for lost doggies, the nice lady took us to meet a doctor friend of hers. She said she just wanted to "show" us to her friend because we were so cute and so sweet. We were also VERY tired.

Mommy said it was love at first sight. When she said, "I'll take them," our hearts burst with joy. She hugged us so tight and said, "Dick and Jane, we are going to be a family." Finally, we had a forever mommy.

Mommy's work friends bought collars, leashes, beds, food, and even treats for us. When we got to our new house, we snuggled together in one of our brand new beds. We were warm and cozy. We were so happy.

When we barked in the middle of the night, Mommy would go outside with us even when it was cold and snowy. She assumed we had to go potty. Little did she know we were more interested in playing tug-of-war. She said, "Go potty. Go potty." We finally did, but playing was much more fun.

The View From The Office

When we got up the next day, Mommy took us to work. We thought her office was very special. There were great big windows and a door leading out to a deck. We saw a river in front of us. It was all frozen and covered with snow. We wanted to play on it, but Mommy said, "No". She said the ice was too thin.

In the spring, we saw ducks, geese and even a blue heron.

Really pretty swans were floating in the river, too. We saw baby swans with their mommy. The daddy swan watched out for them. We don't have a daddy, but that's OK. Our mommy is just fine.

We also saw squirrels and chipmunks running around the deck. We thought it was fun to have stare-downs with the squirrels. Sometimes they won, and sometimes we won. We liked it best when we won.

One night, we heard a strange noise. It was loud and sounded like it was coming from the floor. Mommy and her client were kind of scared, but we weren't. We knew it was just the raccoons we had been playing with earlier. They were babies, too. We also knew we could protect Mommy and her client.

When summer came we saw speed boats pulling kids on inner tubes. The boats went really fast, and the kids screamed REALLY loud! They made so much noise that they couldn't even hear us bark. It looked like so much fun! We wanted to go, too, but they didn't stop for us.

We saw people in boats fishing on the river. We liked to bark at them, too, just so they knew we were there. Mommy said we would scare the fish away. We weren't sure the fish really cared, and the fishermen just kept on fishing.

Every night for thirteen years, we have gone home from the office with Mommy. We eat dinner, give Mommy big kisses (she likes puppy kisses), and snuggle in our beds. We are so lucky. Mommy says she is lucky, too.

The Clients

The people who come to see Mommy are called clients. They need someone to talk to. They are often scared and sad. We remember being scared and sad. It was not fun.

Mommy says laughter is really healing. We are good at making clients laugh. We like to bury our noses in their purses looking for something good to eat. Sometimes we find cough drops or gum before anyone catches us. We especially like bubble gum.

When the session is over, the clients throw their teary tissues in the waste basket. When no one is looking, we get them out and tear them up. We leave some of them on the floor. This is our very own tissue party.

We like to entertain everyone with our singing. You have never heard such harmony out of puppies. We even seem to know when to stop at exactly the same time. Everyone thinks we are hilarious... except those who have a different idea of music.

It is really important to show respect to Mommy's clients. When a client leaves OUR office, we sit at the doorway until Mommy and the client leave. Mommy then turns around and says, "OK." That means we can run down the hallway---so we do! Mommy says we have to wait so we don't knock the clients down.

VALUES

HOPE

LOYALTY

EMPATHY

RESPECT

FUN

HAPPINESS

FRIENDSHIP

LOVE

HUMOR

We have been so busy since we came to live with Mommy. Mommy says we are her four-legged kids. She has two-legged kids, too, and they have kids of their own. That's a lot of kids. She said she taught all of us some important values.

27

Best Friend

Too cute!

My Best Friend

Spoiled Rotten!

In the Dog House

29

The best therapist has fur and four legs

Roseann is a counseling psychologist who works in a small group practice in Elkhart, Indiana. This is the first book she has written. She is working on two Dick and Jane sequels: *Double Trouble with Dick and Jane* and *Senior Living with Dick and Jane.* The books were inspired after many comments were made by clients who love the real Dick and Jane and have benefited from their presence. Roseann has two children and four grandchildren who witness the antics of Dick and Jane. All of them provide love and laughter on a daily basis.

Elena has a passion for illustrating picture books for children. Her illustrations capture the eyes of children and adults alike. Elena uses her gift of art in designing business cards, postcards, posters, banners, and other creative products. She incorporates art in her free time in the form of chalk painting and CG illustrations.

Follow up with Dick and Jane in the upcoming book series.

Double trouble with Dick and Jane.

Senior Living with Dick and Jane.

For more children's books visit our web site

www.marianapublishing.com

Find us on:

 @LlcMariana | @marianapublishing | @marianapublishing

A special thanks goes out to Roger Carlson who coordinated all aspects of writing and publishing this book. There is no way Precious Moments with Dick and Jane could have turned a dream into a reality. Thank you, Roger.

Copyright © 2020 by Mariana Publishing LLC.

All rights reserved, including the right of reproduction in whole or in part in any form.
All rights reserved. This book or any portion thereof may not be reproduced or used in any manner whatsoever without the express written permission of the publisher except for the use of brief excerpts for review purposes.

ISBN: 978-1-64510-026-3 (hardback)
ISBN: 978-1-64510-027-0 (Hardback with Sleeve)
ISBN: 978-1-64510-025-6 (Amazon)
ISBN: 978-1-64510-028-7 (Print on Demand)

First Published in 2020
Printed in the USA